When Thou didst descend to death, O Life Immortal,
Thou didst slay hell with the splendor of Thy Godhead,
And when from the depths Thou didst raise the dead,
All the powers of heaven cried out,
O Giver of life, Christ our God, glory to Thee.
—Resurrectional Troparion (Tone 2)

Be awed today. With trembling look
Upon the tomb of Christ, who took
The sting of death and sin away
And rests within the earth today.

IC
XC
MP
ΘV

Great and Holy Saturday

from ***The Three-Day Pascha*** series

by Mother Melania
with illustrations by Bonnie Gillis

CONCILIAR PRESS
Ben Lomond, California

Great and Holy Saturday
from ***The Three-Day Pascha*** series

Published by Conciliar Press
P.O. Box 76
Ben Lomond, California 95005

Printed in Canada

ISBN 1-888212-80-2

The whole creation wept to see
His death upon the dreadful tree.
The sun in terror hid its face
When Christ God died for Adam's race!

The Theotokos cries, "My Son!
What have the wicked people done?
How could they dare to murder Thee—
Thou God of Love and Majesty?

ΜΡ
ΘΥ

"And now what joy is left for me,
Who have no life apart from Thee?
Since Thou, my Child, hast gone away,
O take me with Thee, Lord, I pray!"

"My dearest Mother, do not weep
To see Me in the tomb asleep
In death," the Lord of all replies,
"For on the third day, I shall rise!"

Note: This icon represents Christ in the tomb. The spear which pierced Christ's side is on His left; the stick on which He was offered vinegar and gall is on the right.

IC
XC

Yes! Death can't conquer Christ, for He
Is God from all eternity,
And by His rising, He shall bring
New life to all created things!

And though He has most truly died,
He has not left His Father's side.
For in the heavens, He still reigns
Though in the grave He now remains.

And while He rests within the grave,
Our God, who came to earth to save,
Releases Hades' captives, who
Through Him are granted life anew.

"No mortal tongue can hope to sing
Thy praises, O my Son and King,"
The Virgin tells her Holy Son,
For by His death, our life is won.

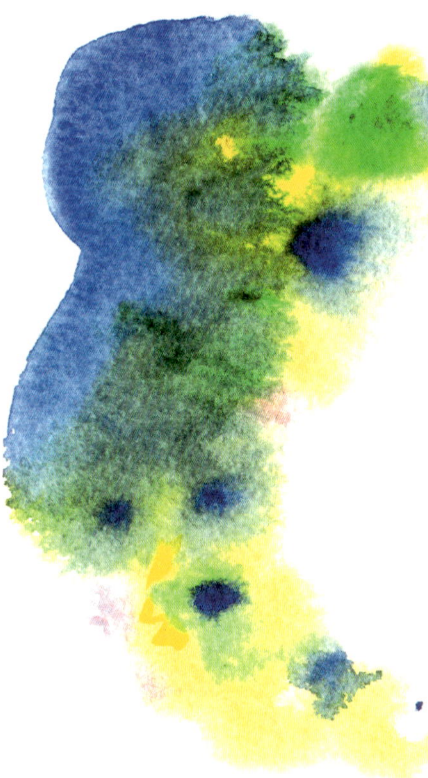

So, now with sad but eager hush
All creatures wait for Thee to crush
The devil's power and to make
Creation new for Thy Name's sake.

Be hushed, then, and in purity
Prepare your heart and soul to see
The Day of Days, the Feast of Feasts —
The Rising of our Great High Priest.

Note: It is a custom in the Byzantine tradition for the priest to scatter bay leaves around the church during the Liturgy on Holy Saturday afternoon.

ABOUT THE AUTHOR AND ILLUSTRATOR:

Mother Melania is a member of the community of St. Barbara Orthodox Monastery in Santa Paula, California. An earlier series of her poems, *The Twelve Feasts for Children,* was published under the name of Sister Elayne, her name before she was professed as a stavrophor nun.

Bonnie Gillis is an iconographer and illustrator. She lives in Langley, British Columbia, Canada, where her husband, Father Michael, is pastor of Holy Nativity Orthodox Mission.

ABOUT THE SERIES:

All of history is the story of God's saving love for fallen man and creation. The Twelve Great Feasts of the Church celebrate great high points in this story, but above them all stands Pascha—the Feast of Feasts. All things either lead to Pascha or flow from it. Pascha is, of course, the Church's traditional name for Easter. It is the "Passover" of Christ—and of us through Him—from death to life. And since Pascha is the "Passover" from death to life, the Church has always seen it as the three-day Pascha. Great and Holy Friday, Great and Holy Saturday, and the Day of Resurrection form a seamless whole. To think of one without the other two is to misunderstand it.

Great and Holy Saturday is *the* Sabbath—the Day of Rest to which all other Sabbaths point. As Christ God rested from the work of creation on the seventh day, now He rests from His work of re-creation, which He finished on Good Friday, the sixth day. It is also the day on which Christ begins to free Hades' captives, the day on which death begins to feel the presence of the Living God. Thus, it is a day of hushed expectation—solemn, yet already deeply joyful. Pascha is almost here!